Eliza's
Cherry Trees

Eliza's Cherry Trees

Japan's Gift to America

By Andrea Zimmerman
Illustrated by Ju Hong Chen

PELICAN PUBLISHING COMPANY
GRETNA 2011

To Aiko Sato, a friend from Japan—A. Z.

With thanks to Daniel Howard Sidmore—A. Z.

The word "Pelican" and the depiction of a pelican are trademarks of Pelican Publishing Company, Inc., and are registered in the U.S. Patent and Trademark Office.

Library of Congress Cataloging-in-Publication Data

Zimmerman, Andrea Griffing.
  Eliza's cherry trees : Japan's gift to America / by Andrea Zimmerman ; illustrated by Ju Hong Chen.
       p. cm.
  ISBN 978-1-58980-954-3 (hardcover : alk. paper) 1. Scidmore, Eliza Ruhamah, 1856-1928—Juvenile literature. 2. Japanese flowering cherry—Washington (D.C.)—History—20th century—Juvenile literature. 3. Diplomatic gifts—Japan—History—20th century—Juvenile literature. 4. Japan—Foreign relations—United States—Juvenile literature. 5. United States—Foreign relations—Japan—Juvenile literature. 6. Urban beautification—Washington (D.C.)—History—20th century—Juvenile literature. I. Chen, Ju-Hong. II. Title.

SB413.C5Z56 2011
975.3'03092—dc22
[B]

2010046163

Printed in Singapore
Published by Pelican Publishing Company, Inc.
1000 Burmaster Street, Gretna, Louisiana 70053

ELIZA'S CHERRY TREES:
JAPAN'S GIFT TO AMERICA

Sometimes a person with a good idea can make a big difference. Eliza Scidmore was one of those people. She changed America's capital, Washington, D.C.

Eliza and her brother grew up in her mother's boarding house in Washington. It was a lively place. Eliza met many politicians and travelers who stayed there. Eliza's mother was even friends with President Abraham Lincoln and his wife. Eliza got to visit them and play at the White House.

One of Eliza's best subjects at school was geography. She liked studying the world and all the countries in it. Eliza loved Washington, but she wanted to visit the real places on her maps. Eliza wanted to see the world.

In those days, few people could travel away from home. Eliza was lucky—her mother took her to Europe when she was a teenager. She saw fascinating new places.

In 1873 Eliza went away to college. She liked writing and she was good at it. She was starting to feel grown up, and she liked being independent. Women at that time had very few choices. Eliza had different ideas. She didn't think she had to stay home and be a wife, or be a teacher or a nurse like many other women.

Eliza wanted to keep traveling, so she had to find a way.

After college, Eliza started writing articles for the newspaper. She worked hard and made good money. Soon Eliza was paying her own way for her travels.

When she was twenty-six, Eliza bought tickets to faraway Alaska. Few tourists had ever been there. Eliza wrote reports for the newspapers back home. She loved sharing the fascinating things she saw, such as huge glaciers, spouting whales, and the native people. Eliza even wrote a book—the first guidebook about Alaska.

When Eliza went back to Washington, it wasn't long before she started thinking about traveling again. She decided to visit her older brother, who was working in Japan. Eliza sailed across the ocean.

In Japan, she rode on trains, carriages, and bumpy rickshaws. She climbed mountains, ate strange foods, and visited ancient temples. Everything was so different! She studied Japanese art and learned to speak Japanese. She fell in love with Japan and its people.

Eliza especially loved Japanese gardens. Eliza's favorite plants, by far, were the Japanese cherry trees. Eliza called them "the most beautiful thing in the world." Thousands of the trees were planted in parks and along the riverbanks. When they bloomed, the trees became clouds of pink blossoms. As the petals drifted down, it was like pink snowfall. The Japanese people loved the cherry trees as their national symbol. Crowds gathered for picnics under the trees. People wrote poems and painted pictures to honor those *sakura*.

When Eliza came back home, she wrote a book about Japan. She wanted to share her love of Japan with other Americans. She wanted the nations of Japan and America to be friends.

Even though she was always thinking about her next journey, Eliza loved coming home to Washington, D.C. She was proud of America's growing capital and wanted it to look as beautiful as any city in the world.

She thought about the muddy land from a recent construction project in the swampy area around the riverbank. Eliza had a wonderful idea. She remembered the beautiful cherry trees in Japan. She thought, "That's what Washington needs!"

Eliza told the man in charge of the Washington parks about the wonderful cherry trees. She showed him photographs that she had taken. She told him about her plan to plant hundreds of cherry trees down by the water. He said no. He believed that they didn't need any different kind of tree in Washington.

But Eliza knew that sometimes when you have a good idea, you have to keep trying. So she waited. When a new parks man was hired, she told him about her good idea. He, too, said no.

Eliza kept traveling. She also met with friends who loved to travel. Some of these friends had started the National Geographic Society. The society was for people who wanted to learn more about the world.

Eliza was the first woman to have an important job there, and she helped the society grow. She wrote many articles and books. Eliza made more trips to Japan, Alaska, and Europe, and she explored India, China, Russia, and Java, an island of Indonesia.

Eliza also became a photographer. Not many women did that, either. She took pictures for the Smithsonian Institution and recorded people and places that Americans had never seen.

But Eliza didn't forget about the cherry trees, and she didn't give up. She kept trying for more than twenty years! Every time a new man was hired to be in charge of the parks department, Eliza went to tell him about her idea. Each one said no.

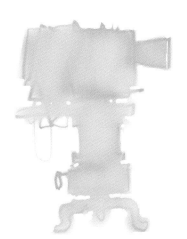

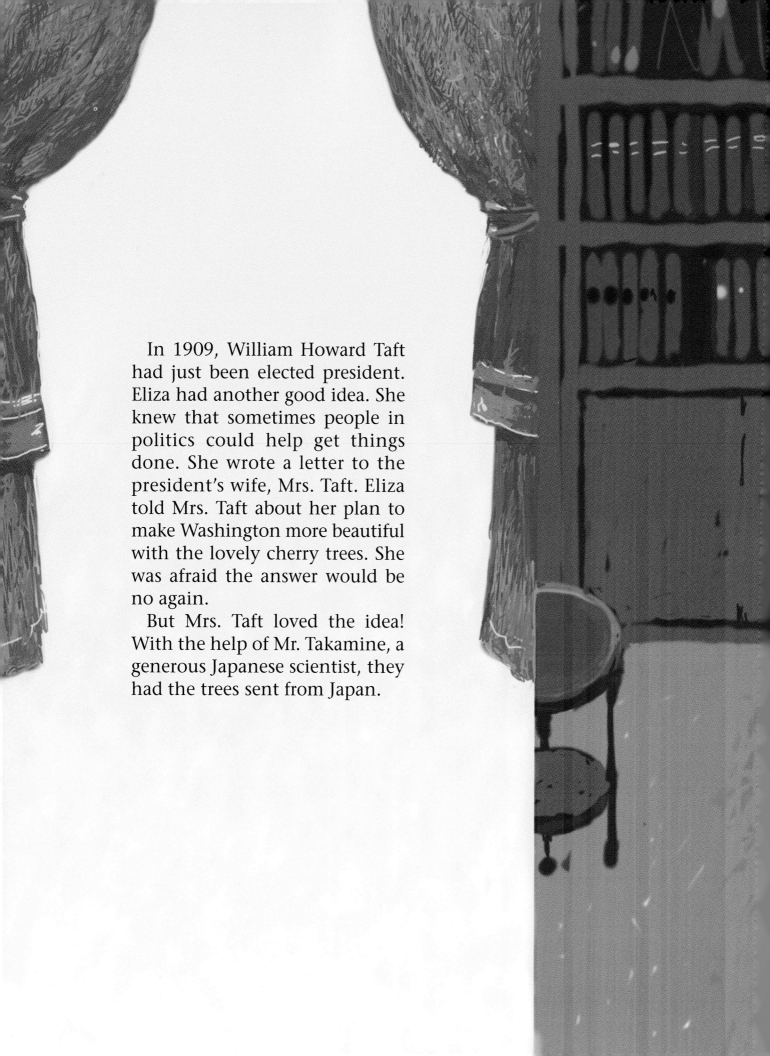

In 1909, William Howard Taft had just been elected president. Eliza had another good idea. She knew that sometimes people in politics could help get things done. She wrote a letter to the president's wife, Mrs. Taft. Eliza told Mrs. Taft about her plan to make Washington more beautiful with the lovely cherry trees. She was afraid the answer would be no again.

But Mrs. Taft loved the idea! With the help of Mr. Takamine, a generous Japanese scientist, they had the trees sent from Japan.

Everyone was happily waiting for the trees to arrive. Eliza imagined the beautiful pink clouds of blossoms that would soon be blooming in Washington.

In January of 1910, two thousand cherry trees arrived. They were given as a gift from Japan's capital city, Tokyo. But there was a problem. The trees had diseases and bugs. The inspectors were afraid they would make American trees sick. The president agreed. He signed an order for all the cherry trees to be burned to ashes.

Eliza was so disappointed. She was also afraid that the Japanese people would be offended. But the mayor of Tokyo said they understood. He even joked about George Washington chopping down a cherry tree.

New trees were carefully grown in Japan. In March of 1912, three thousand new trees arrived. They were inspected and declared healthy!

On March 27, 1912, there was a small ceremony at the planting of the first two cherry trees. Eliza watched as her longtime dream was finally coming true.

Over the years, the trees grew, and every spring, they bloomed. People began gathering to enjoy them and to celebrate their beauty, just like in Japan. Eliza was happy to see how they helped turn Washington, D.C. into one of the most beautiful cities in the world.

As she grew older, Eliza remembered all the places she had visited. She believed that all the countries in the world could live together in peace. She spent her later years working for that. She knew that sometimes, when you have a good idea, you just have to keep trying for a long time.

Eliza was very happy that her lovely Japanese cherry trees in Washington, D.C. became an international symbol of peace and friendship.

ELIZA RUHAMAH SCIDMORE
(pronounced "Sid-more")

October 14, 1856: Eliza was born in Clinton, Iowa. She was called "Lillie" by her family.

ca. 1861: At about age five, Eliza and her older brother George moved to Washington, D.C. with their mother. Eliza grew up and went to school there.

1873-75: Eliza attended Oberlin College in Ohio.

1876: Eliza started writing society columns for the newspapers.

1883: Eliza visited Alaska for the first time.

1885: Eliza's first book, *Alaska Its Southern Coast and the Sitkan Archipelago,* was published. It was based on travel articles she wrote for the newspapers.

1885: Eliza returned from her first visit to Japan, where her brother worked as an American diplomat. Eliza proposed that Japanese cherry trees should be planted along the reclaimed land by the riverbank to the Washington, D.C. parks supervisor. She continued to propose the plan during the next twenty-four years.

1890: Eliza joined the new National Geographic Society. For more than two decades, she contributed work as a writer, editor, photographer, lecturer, and member of the Board of Managers.

1891: Her book about Japan, *Jinrikisha Days in Japan,* was published.

1905-08: Eliza's friend, Dr. David Fairchild, planted Japanese cherry trees in the Washington, D.C. area to prove that they would grow well there.

April 1909: Eliza wrote to Helen Taft explaining her idea for the cherry trees to be planted and Mrs. Taft agreed to help. Dr. Jokichi Takamine offered to pay for the trees.

January 1910: The first shipment of two thousand trees arrived, but they were destroyed due to disease.

March 1912: The second shipment of more than three thousand healthy trees arrived.

March 27, 1912: The ceremonial planting of the cherry trees took place in Potomac Park.

1923: Eliza moved to Switzerland.

November 3, 1928: Eliza died in Geneva, Switzerland. Her ashes were taken to Japan and buried in Yokohama.

Eliza was truly a world traveler, especially in Europe and Asia. In addition to her books on Alaska and Japan, she wrote books about traveling in India, China, Java, and Korea.